The Secrets to Buildin

"Ed has compiled a body of wisdom founded on entrepreneurs' real-life experiences. Practicing the guidance provided by this body of professionals and entrepreneurs will highly increase your probability of success. Ed takes these lessons a step further by adding his own personal experiences to help MBEs operate outside of the box on their journeys to building successful minority-owned businesses."

—Fernando Martinez, President and CEO, Northwest Mountain Minority Supplier Development Council

"This book is an inspiring reminder that the path to your destiny already lies within you! These tips remind us that moving from good to great, while often painful, is in fact the journey to success. This book shares the lived experiences minority entrepreneurs must embark upon to get to the other side that awaits them if they are patient and prepared."

—Judson Robinson III, President, Houston Area Urban League

"I highly recommend every minority business owner read this book. It is a handbook that every minority owner can always refer to; it is also an inspiring book, in which Ed uses his personal story and experiences to teach others how to become a true leader, with the right attitude and persistence. Having been a minority business owner for many years, I have faced similar challenges to the ones mentioned by Ed. Through reading the book, I was touched by Ed's passion, thought leadership, and integrity, which are the reasons why he is such a successful minority business owner."

—Bin Yu, Board Chair, Asian Chamber of Commerce, Houston

THE SECRETS TO BUILDING A SUCCESSFUL MINORITY-OWNED COMPANY

Joy,

Thank you for your support. All the best!

Ed Ryland

10-12-19

THE SECRETS TO BUILDING A SUCCESSFUL MINORITY-OWNED COMPANY

Powerful Insights from Minority Business Owners on How to Start, Keep, and Grow a Successful Minority-Owned Business

By Ed Ryland

Copyright © By Ed Ryland

All rights reserved. No part of this book may be reproduced or used in any manner without written permission of the copyright owner except for the use of quotations in a book review.

Other initiatives by Ed Ryland include Debunking the Myth, IMOC (Invest In My Own Community), and the Houston Minority Supplier Development Council's CEO Academy.

To learn more about the author, please visit www.EdRyland.com.

To my late mother, Anna Ryland, and my late wife, Mary Ann Ryland, who never stopped supporting and believing in me. For many years, you kept reminding me that honesty and hard work would pay off. Now it has. I feel your support and presence every day. Thank you.

Thank you to the many MBE's (minority business enterprises) who have contributed to this book. Your time and your thoughtful responses will impact MBEs and make a difference in their lives for years to come.

"I can never beat GOD's giving. The more I give, the more I am blessed."

—A quote from my mom that I live by

Contents

About the Author..3
Introduction..9
1. Becoming Great..11
2. Only Thirty-Five Dollars to My Name...........................19
3. What Successful Minority-Owned Businesses
Do to Succeed Where Others Fail..................................22
4. Words of Wisdom from Minority Business Owners....30
5. MBEs: Strong as the Golden Gate Bridge..................34
6. A Lesson on Humility—A Key Component of Success.............37
7. Wise Counsel from a Strong Leader...........................41
8. From the Eleventh Floor to the Lobby........................46
9. Nine Key Tips for MBE Success..................................56
10. Iconic MBEs...59
11. More Words of Wisdom from Minority Business Owners........63
12. Executive-Level Insights on MBE Success...............66
13. Even More Words of Wisdom from Minority
Business Owners..70
14. So What Are My Secrets to Success?......................76
15. Closing Thoughts..79
Book Ed Ryland for Speaking Engagements or Events................82
Your Notes and Action Plan...83

About the Author

Ed Ryland, CCIM, MCR, is a successful minority business owner and is recognized as an expert commercial real estate advisor, thought leader, speaker, community game changer, and entrepreneur. He is the founder, president, chairman, and CEO of ARVO Realty Advisors, a successful and highly respected full-service commercial real estate firm based in Houston, Texas. ARVO Realty Advisors works with corporations, government agencies, nonprofit organizations, and small businesses in the areas of consulting, acquisition, disposition, and landlord and tenant representations. A partial list of ARVO's clients includes: Macy's, Shell, EY, Marathon Oil, Hewlett-Packard and the City of Houston.

Prior to founding ARVO Realty Advisors, Ed obtained corporate and government experience through his work with Beneficial Finance and the State of Texas. A passionate entrepreneur, he has launched various other business ventures. First, Ed cofounded Concordis Real Estate, the first national minority-owned commercial real estate firm addressing corporate America's lack of diversity in commercial real estate. He has since mentored and guided hundreds of MBEs. Second, Ed founded Debunking the Myth, a conference focused on the stereotypes preventing development in underserved and underdeveloped communities. Third, Ed founded IMOC (Invest In My Own Community). This unique program educates and gives power to those who live and work in underserved communities, helping them to create generational wealth through commercial real estate and community involvement. Fourth, Ed created the Economic Development and Diversity Institute for the Houston

Association of Realtors. Fifth, Ed is responsible for the Houston Minority Development Council's CEO Academy idea. This program exposes minority business owners to CEOs of major corporations, strategic thinking, and leadership.

Ed is a sought-after public speaker on topics including diversity, commercial real estate, and youth and community groups. Ed has been featured on televised programs such as *Houston Life,* as well as featured in the *Houston Business Journal,* the *Houston Forward Times,* the *Houston Chronicle,* and the *Houston Defender.* He served as the first African American executive team member for the Houston Association of Realtors, the largest real estate association in the country.

He is a graduate of Leadership Houston and a fellow at the Center for Houston's Future. He is also a past president of both the Houston Real Estate Association (HREA) and the Texas Association of Real Estate Brokers (TAREB). Ed is a graduate of the Dartmouth College Tuck School of Business MBE Executive Program and the Northwestern University Kellogg School of Management Advanced Management Education Program. Ed holds the CCIM (Certified Commercial Investment Member) designation, recognized as the PhD of commercial real estate, and earned the Master of Corporate Real Estate (MCR) diploma from CoreNet, the country's premier corporate real estate organization. Ed serves as national vice chair of the National Minority Supplier Development Council's (NMSDC) Minority Input Committee.

In 2019, Ed received the Lifetime Achievement Award from CoreNet Houston and the Larry V. Green Community Leadership Award from the Texas Black Expo. Ed maintains active involvement in community service. He is a proud member of Big Brothers Big Sisters, the Greater Houston Black Chamber, CoreNet, CCIM, the Houston Black Real Estate Association, the Houston Minority Supplier Development Council, and the International Council of Shopping Centers (ICSC).

Ed does considerable work with community-based organizations. His leadership of IMOC (Invest In My Own Community) examined the role of fear and mystery on creating generational wealth through commercial real estate for underserved underinvested communities. Ed is a former member of the board of directors for CoreNet Houston and current chair of Prairie View A&M University's College of Business advisory board.

Ed was born in St. Louis, Missouri, the son of the late Anna Vasser Ryland and Edward Ryland Sr., and raised in North St. Louis along with his sister, Delores, who is now also a real estate professional. He currently resides in Houston, Texas, where he was married to Mary Ann Ryland before her passing in May 2017.

They are both proud parents of their two daughters, Tiffany and Stephanie, and son, Aubrey, as well as proud grandparents to their granddaughter, Amya. Ed is a member of St. John's United Methodist Church in Houston and firmly believes that "we are blessed to be a blessing."

OTHER AWARDS AND INVOLVEMENT:

- 2019, Larry V. Green Community Leadership Award from the Texas Black Expo
- 2019, CoreNet Houston Lifetime Achievement Award
- March 2, 2018, CoreNet Global Master of Corporate Real Estate (MCR)
- 2016, Houston's Best and Brightest Companies to Work For
- May 2015, Houston Community College Procurement Review Committee
- May 2012, Certificate of Appreciation from the Albright Middle School Annual Career Day
- December 14, 2011, Houston Minority Supplier Development Council MBE to MBE Development Award
- September 24, 2011, Inaugural Class of Goldman Sachs 10,000 Small Businesses Program
- Houston Citizens Chamber of Commerce 2011 Pinnacle Award Winner

- 2010, Alief Family YMCA Appreciation Award
- 2007, Marathon Oil Corporation Living Our Values Award, Finalist
- August 25, 2006, US Department of Commerce Regional Minority Business Services Firm of the Year
- December 15, 2005, Houston Minority Business Council Board of Directors presentation, "In Honor of Ed Ryland for the Time, Dedication support and Leadership to the Houston Minority Business Council as Chair of the Minority Business Enterprise Advisory Committee"
- 2005, Presenter for National Black MBA Association, Houston Chapter, "Owning the Dream"
- 2004, Emerging 10 Award by the Houston Minority Business Council
- June 10, 2003, Certificate of Achievement, Creating Leadership in Action by Leadership Houston
- May 22, 2003, Federal Bureau of Investigation, Houston Division, FBI Citizens Academy Program
- 2002–2007 Houston Minority Business Council Board of Directors, Treasurer and MBE Advisory Committee Chair
- 2000, First Small Business Chairperson for Houston's Government Procurement Connections (GPC)
- 2000–2001 Shell Youth Training Academy Mentor
- July 2001, Minority Business Executive
- November 6, 1998, Texas Association of Real Estate Brokers Meritorious Award
- April 1998, Certificate of Accomplishment, Community MBA administered by the College and Graduate School of Business at The University of Texas at Austin
- June 11, 1994, Outstanding Leadership Award presented by Texas Realtist
- July 1993, Businessperson of the Month by the Guaranty Federal Bank FSB and the Houston Defender.
- 1993–1994, Business Professionals of America
- Houston Business and Professional Men's Club

- 1992–1993 Houston Real Estate Association, Award for Excellent Guidance and Dedicated Services
- 1990, Realtist of The Year
- West Houston Chamber of Commerce Board Member
- Houston Minority Supplier Development Council, MBE to MBE Development Award
- Discover Leadership Training Master Graduate

Introduction

By Richard Huebner, former president of the Houston Minority Supplier Development Council

I have had the pleasure of calling Ed Ryland my good friend for more than thirty years. I first met him in my capacity as president of the Houston Minority Supplier Development Council (HMSDC) when he was president of the Black Realtors Association. Ed immediately impressed me as an articulate, determined, and capable leader. Since that time, I have worked closely with Ed in his roles as a member, committee chair, program manager, award winner, and officer of the National Minority Supplier Development Council's Minority Business Enterprise Input Committee, and as a director and treasurer of the board of directors of the HMSDC.

To say that Ed Ryland is one of the most likeable, respected, and successful entrepreneurs is an understatement. Ed chose the field of commercial real estate as his desired profession, knowing full well that there were very few minorities in that field. His ability and determination enabled him to count as his customers today some of the world's leading corporations, such as Marathon Oil, Walmart, Macy's, Hewlett-Packard, and many more. Ed was recently recognized with a Lifetime Achievement Award by CoreNet, perhaps the leading global corporate commercial real estate organization.

Ed was always inspired by the examples of other minority business owners. At every opportunity, Ed would ask about the owners' experiences and lessons learned. Ed and I played tennis together regularly. On every occasion, Ed would bring along a list of business questions. We ended up spending more time courtside on his questions than we did playing tennis! Ed and I traveled together extensively for years on behalf of the National Minority Supplier Development Council. Again, Ed came prepared with his questions for the plane trip or over cigars late at night, and he would meet with his fellow minority business owners at every chance he had so he could explore their experiences and hear their concerns. Ed would contemplate what he learned from these entrepreneurs and what he could incorporate into his business to drive its success. Then, Ed would stay one or two additional days to build his network, ultimately giving him a national and international capability to help earn him the clients listed above.

Ed is a giver. His faith, his family, his employees, and his success aside, nothing delights Ed more than to see a minority business owner succeed as a result of something Ed said or the example he set for others. Thus, he created this book, *The Secrets to Building a Successful Minority-Owned Company*. Ed wants to share his own personal experiences and learnings, as well as the lessons learned by countless other minority business owners, in the hope that this book will help you achieve similar success in your business and in your personal life.

So, enjoy this book and use it to grow yourself and your business as another profoundly successful minority-owned business!

1
BECOMING GREAT

In the book *Good to Great: Why Some Companies Make the Leap . . . And Others Don't*, author Jim Collins states that good is the enemy of great. In his view, the vast majority of companies never become great precisely because they become quite good—and then allow themselves to stay at that level instead of striving ahead. That is why so few companies break through to become truly great. He asks, "Can a good company become a great company, and if so, how?" That's precisely the question I've asked myself as I've explored the secrets of building a successful minority-owned company. One of the keys to building a successful minority-owned company is to learn from the experiences of others, and then take those experiences in order to go from being a good minority-owned company to a great company—PERIOD! You will find that kind of advice in this book.

In order to build a great minority-owned company, you have to have the right leaders—leaders who possess the ability to think of others more than they think of themselves, leaders who lead by example

> **Here are the FACTS**
>
> • 8 million of the 28 million small businesses in the United States are minority-owned
>
> • Of those 8 million, 2.6 million are African American–owned
>
> • 3.3 million are Hispanic-owned
>
> Average Annual Revenue:
> - Afro American: $58,119
> - Hispanic: $143,271
> - Asian: $364,717
> - Nonminority: $552,079
>
> **WHY?** Our goal is to turn 500,000 failing. fledgling minority-owned firms into thriving successful businesses by December 31, 2020, and to ensure that future minority entrepreneurs have extraordinary success.

without expecting attention or applause, leaders who have the ability to produce extraordinary results, leaders who will not tolerate mediocre performance, and leaders who position their successors for even greater success.

You never reach the finish line unless you start. As I presented this project to current and future minority business owners, I have been blessed by a host of friends, family, associates, and minority business owners who have followed my path to success from the very beginning. We set out to bring you the best information you could find on building a successful minority-owned company. My daughters Tiffany and Stephanie have been there every step of the way. Their love for me and for this project made the challenging times easier to get through. To those minority business owners who came before me and unselfishly gave of their time and resources so that other minority-owned companies would be better for it, we say thank you. And finally, thanks to my staff who made it possible for me to pursue this adventure. I'm lucky to have you.

I can remember my decision to launch my own firm as if it were yesterday. I recall the questions I asked myself. I had had a very successful year working for another real estate firm. Although by most standards I was successful, something was still missing. I had felt myself being pulled toward entrepreneurship for several years.

As I left my office, I began thinking about how I would present the idea to my wife, Mary Ann. I already knew that she would support it, but I wanted her to be a part of the decision since I recognized that life as we knew it would most likely change, for sure in the short term. As for me, my mind was fixated on building the premier real estate firm in Houston, Texas. I had watched owners of real estate firms for several years, observing their style, their ability to manage people, their vision, and their leadership skills. I was fortunate to be in a position to benchmark where I was and where I wanted to go. After receiving the news, my wife—as only she could say it, in a way that made me feel like I could accomplish anything—said, "If that's what you want to do, do it." She never doubted me or stopped supporting me or my ideal. It is through that strength that I grabbed a recorder and began the journey to write this book, *The Secrets to Building a Successful Minority-Owned Company*. Hearing about the pain, challenges, successes, and impact of other minority business leaders inspired me to write this book. I have always been curious about and attracted to what makes individuals and companies successful. I have studied and interviewed top performers and business leaders in various fields. I have read hundreds of books, but I have never seen a book pinpointing what makes a minority business successful. My focus has shifted from reading and interviewing to sharing and writing about those ideas and strategies that truly epitomize the minority business spirit. These are the stories of skilled, insightful, innovative game changers. I had the honor of talking to, listening to, and interviewing minority business owners from across the country in various businesses. I was allowed to pull from a fountain of endless wisdom. While I have accumulated my own experiences as a minority business owner, others have offered rich, valuable insights that cannot be understated. They have been there, and they generously share their secrets here. My primary purpose is to galvanize a collection of rich ideas in a way that is easy to understand and implement, and to have current and future minority entrepreneurs saying, "I can do that." What's interesting is that the ideas shared were as relevant when I started my firm over 30 years ago as they are today. These are everyday individuals who have a tremendous work ethic and a commitment to rising early, staying late, and filling their days by managing all sorts of issues in-between and finding valuable solutions.

Some are serial entrepreneurs who have tried and failed and now are succeeding. Some are second- and third-generation business owners. I was struck by their spiritual connections and strong moral compasses, grounded in humility. I presented each person with the same question: "What do you think it takes to be a successful minority business owner?" They spoke with straightforward dialogue, tapping into their personal experiences about what they would tell the next generation, what advice they were given, and what got them through the difficult times. Their stories have impacted their sons and daughters, and perhaps will impact yours. In this way, the minority business community will continue doing for those less fortunate—truly making a generational impact, so that future aspiring minority business owners really believe that they are priceless and created for a purpose. You can do anything and be anything if you are willing and prepared to make the sacrifices. One thing came through loud and clear throughout my interviews: Never give up. Keep dreaming. Keep pursuing your destiny. I asked, "If you only have one to two minutes to share your secrets of success to other minority business owners, what would you say? What changed the course of your business and life? What's important to you? What is your recipe?" Countless minority entrepreneurs from every ethnic and gender background gave selflessly of their time to contribute their stories that speak of courage, aspiration, hope, triumph, and success. They shared how to navigate the challenging pathways of minority entrepreneurship. Some were financially independent and some were pushing their way through difficult times. They were attorneys, CPAs, manufacturers, real estate professionals, logistics experts, ranchers, marketers, engineers, physicians, project managers, IT consultants, and the list goes on. I felt honored and privileged as they openly shared. I was touched by the story of one minority business owner as he shared about how his grandfather started the company on a hope and a dream, and now they are one of the largest MBEs in the country, with multiple divisions and companies. I had an opportunity to interview a father-and-son team, and just listening and watching that interaction was amazing. I saw the pride in the father as he stepped back as to say, "Son, you are in charge now." At the same time, I watched the son speak with such confidence and respect about what his dad had done. This is generational legacy-building in action. It's no surprise that faith and spirituality seem to be a part of most minority business owners' stories. Within these pages, you will find the words of a war veteran and automobile pioneer who endured unbelievable challenges as he built and passed on his successful minority-owned company. This should be an inspiration to any business owner. Your emotions will be stirred by the blood, sweat, and tears given to build their companies. These secrets of success are a testimony to the fact that minorities bring a unique ability to succeed and provide extraordinary solutions.

These secrets came not only from US firms, but from companies in places as far away as South Africa. You could see and feel the pain, joy, success, and pride in their faces as they described their journeys to success. Several asked, "What is this for?" When I shared that we wanted to capture what makes MBEs successful and to share that with others, they all said, "That's a great idea." I sat around a table with six minority business owners and supplier diversity professionals during breakfast, and we had an open dialogue about what makes minority business owners successful. Representatives from small, start-up companies and large, mature companies alike were talking candidly about their businesses, what they did, and what they needed to grow their businesses and build capacity. Various languages were spoken, so you had to listen closely to clearly understand the powerful information they were sharing. Some time later, as I was walking the halls of a national conference, the National Minority Supplier Development Conference, I observed people from many ethnic groups and businesses who were proudly pounding the floors, shaking hands, giving elevator pitch after elevator pitch, and refining their value propositions. Some were new and nervous. Others had done it a thousand times. Many were colleagues, whose friendships had developed over the past 30 years. You could see that some were moving slower and that the daily and yearly grind had physically taken its toll. There they were in the true minority business owner spirit, shaking hands, offering advice, and continuing to fight. That's what I love about the minority business community. As I stood back and scanned the crowd, there were new faces, but there were some missing faces, like my good friend, the late Ron Williams. Ron fought tirelessly for minorities and made a tremendous contribution that will impact MBEs for many years. I could not leave God out of the equation. God was at work here helping me to identify and tap into some of the brightest business minds in the country. The words and thoughts of this unique group of leaders were amazing, intertwining highly educated book sense with hands-on street sense. Some of the best advice did not come from those with PhDs, but from ordinary people who just decided to go for it. These courageous MBEs teach us, once again, the importance of faith, perseverance, honesty, integrity, and respect. Many shared the events that determined the course of their lives. They spoke of the impact of their parents and grandparents. To paraphrase my uncle Scott, who owned a janitorial company, a shoe shining business, a hauling company, and a used furniture store, "You got to have some excitement in what you do, treat people fairly, and make them feel good about doing business with you." He was a serial minority entrepreneur before the term existed, and he has had the greatest impact on the way I conduct business today.

You may be wondering what you can really gain from the wisdom shared by these brave minority business owners. The answer is clear. Sometimes those best suited for your success are not those who have studied it, but those who have lived it and have the scars to show. In many cases, the quickest and most effective course to success is knowing who and what to follow. Time is one of the most valuable assets we have, and the truth is none of us know how much of it we have left. However long we have left is not enough. A meaningful, deep conversation with someone who has traveled the road you have chosen is priceless. We owe a lot to those who have blazed the trail before us and are willing to share. In today's climate, with all of the overwhelming obstacles facing the minority business community and where some are worried and uncertain about their future as a MBE, the wisdom, words, and inspiration offered by other minority business owners becomes critically important. *The Secrets to Building a Successful Minority-Owned Company* is designed to be an easy, real-life resource and a tool addressing entrepreneurs' most concerning questions and struggles. The pathway to your business success lies between these pages. How, then, shall you use them? The words and thoughts from these geniuses can unlock your success and impact the lifestyle of your family for generations to come. This is not just information you read once and then set on the shelf. It's meant for you to keep handy and reference when things are going well, as well as when you encounter a struggle. Most importantly, we hope you share this book with other minority business owners or aspiring minority business owners. The central message is that you can do it, whatever your "it" is. Read any of the many comments or stories, and absorb and meditate on the encouraging messages and strategies until you have your "Aha!" moment. Keep an open mind, and be willing to challenge conventional wisdom and your own thinking. If you are like me, you have read hundreds or thousands of books searching for the right words or answers to address our inadequacies. This book offers some solutions to help you navigate the minority business owner's most challenging decisions. The wisdom found between these pages will help you meet the dilemmas of the day and develop your own customized solutions. For so many of us, despair sometimes seems to be all around. If you meditate on the wise counsel contained on these pages, you will find inspiration and sufficiency, as well as a warehouse of ideas to empower you.

Now it's time for you to relax and prepare to enjoy hundreds of years of the minority businesses journey to success. Picture yourself in their place: developing your strategy, hitting a brick wall, overcoming that challenge, and building a great company, making a difference for your community and the world. These brave MBEs understand their calling well. You cannot have a conversation with them without feeling their commitment and their undeniable love for their community and the MBE family. Their foundational approach to solving any problem rests in these simple principles: God, education, and hard work. The most successful MBEs exemplified authentic humility; for them it was about eliminating all the excuses, even in the worst of times. I hope you are encouraged, empowered, and destined to run the MBE race no matter what. If you are, your story can be added to those who know how to build a successful minority-owned business.

2
Only Thirty-Five Dollars to My Name

There I was on a steamy summer night in Houston, Texas. The streetlights had just come on, and the mosquitoes were biting badly. I just finished a long day in the office, frustrated and concerned because the business was not going as I thought it should. At that time, my neighbors would come out and we would have a conversation about life. This was the worst financial time of my life. Here I was, an entrepreneur with a family, three kids, a mortgage, employees, and a company to run.

My car had long since stopped running, so I was driving my wife's tan Mazda 929. It was a beautiful car when we first bought it, and it had been her pride and joy. But now we had driven it so much that the wheels were almost falling off. I can still see and smell it now: the sizzle of the oil dripping and burning on the engine and the odor of antifreeze. I would not dare drive it unless I had two gallons of water and three quarts of oil in the trunk because it was leaking terribly. The automatic windows were no longer working and would not stay up, so I had to use a door stopper to keep the windows up. The lock to open the door from the inside was no longer working either, so I had to reach my arm outside of the window and open the door from the outside. But first, I had to remove the door stopper and slowly ease the window down, being careful not to let it fall all the way between the cracks of the door. If this happened, it was a major challenge to pull the window back up. I did get pretty good at it, though. I was so embarrassed about my car that I would park it blocks from any event I was attending and walk the rest of the way, praying that no one would ask me for a ride.

This particular night, I was going to meet some friends. I drove the 929 a short distance across the street, intending just to stay a little while and chat with my neighbors. We had a good conversation. Afterward, I got back in my car to leave and it would not start, nor could I shift the gears. This was the closest I ever came to saying, "God, why me? You know I only have thirty-five dollars in my pocket and there's no other money anywhere."

The emotions began to build up and I really wanted to cry, but I had to be strong, or at least I thought I did, around my neighbors and family. I could feel my heart beating faster and my chest rising as I began to breathe heavier and harder. This is when one's faith either kicks in or it doesn't. This is a defining moment. I felt myself crying out to God saying, "God, please, please, please help me."

It was about this time that my next-door neighbor, a very good auto mechanic, walked over and asked, "What's wrong?" When you have faith, believe and never give up (never, ever give up), God will put the people and things in your life to take care of you. I began to explain to him the problem with this raggedy-ass car. He calmly said, "Let me take a look at it." In a matter of minutes, he had pushed a couple of buttons and started the car.

Days later I was talking to my mom, sharing as I always did about how I was doing. Regardless of how things were going, I would always say I was doing okay so that I wouldn't worry her. As you know, moms have a way of knowing the truth. Although I never wanted her to worry, on this particular day something told me to share with her what was going on. All I remember is that I started crying over the phone, telling her I just didn't understand. I was working hard and praying hard and doing the things that I thought I needed to do. During this time my wife and I would hold hands and pray in the office on a regular basis, thanking God and asking for his guidance and strength.

I'm getting teary-eyed now just thinking about that conversation with my mom. In her calm, still voice she said, "Baby, everybody needs help every now and then." Days later I received a check for one thousand dollars from my mom. I've never had another thirty-five dollar day since.

Our company has completed multimillion-dollar transactions. We now represent *Fortune* 50 corporations; federal, state and local governments; and some of the most successful small businesses in the country. We have completed transactions in Perth, Australia; Warsaw, Poland; Alaska; and in many states across the country. If you are a minority-owned firm, or aspiring to be a minority-owned firm, hold on, keep the faith, never give up, and take the wisdom from these pages so you will never have to experience a thirty-five dollar day.

3

What Successful Minority-Owned Businesses Do to Succeed Where Others Fail

By Richard Huebner, former president of the Houston Minority Supplier Development Council and one of most recognized experts on building minority-owned businesses

Having helped and observed thousands of businesses over the past thirty-five years, I have noticed some commonalities among those businesses that achieve the most success. Keep the following in mind if you want to grow a successful minority-owned business.

Know your value proposition and impact.

Sure, you need to be able to succinctly describe your product or service so your customer understands what you are bringing to the table. You must also be able to answer the question, "Why you?" How does your product or service relate to the needs of your customer? What distinguishes you from your competition? When asked what you do, do you describe your product or service, or do you explain the results that your customer and others receive as a result of what you do? Your value proposition is the value your product or service has to your customer and the greater good. Goods and services can be obtained from many alternate sources. Value is your opportunity to separate yourself from your competition. How does using you make it better for your customer, your company, your community, and the world? That is impact. Supplier diversity is moving from just counting numbers and dollars to measuring the full impact of using one supplier versus another. Be able to articulate and quantify your impact, where possible. Numbers and metrics give your word both clarity and credibility. Statements that cannot be substantiated are only opinions.

Know where you are headed.

To be a successful leader, you have to be able to clearly articulate where you are going, and you have to have followers (i.e., your customers, employees, banker, colleagues, etc.). If people know where you are going and your plan to get there (e.g., your vision, strategic plan, and operational plan), they can see where they can fit into your plan and help you achieve your vision. Your customers want to know that you will be around for a while before they will take the risk of doing business with you. They will want to know that you have a growth plan before considering you as a long-term supplier and partner. What is your vision, your strategic plan, your business and operational plan? They both define you and guide you to success.

Know your market.

Entrepreneurs often make the mistake of fishing the entire lake at once while using the same bait, instead of finding specific hot spots and using appropriate lures for the fish you are trying to catch. It is important that you know your market and are seen as an expert in that market. What is your specialty? Who are your prospective customers that use this specialty? What special needs do they have? Where do those customers hang out? What do they need to see in you to take you seriously? What are the current trends and changes occurring in your market? These are just a few of the questions you should be asking as you zero in on your market. The answers to these questions give you focus to pinpoint customers and their needs.

Position yourself for success.

It's been said that it is not who you know that counts, but who knows you. Your goal as a supplier is to be the first company that comes to mind when a need for your product or service arises. Another common phrase is out of sight, out of mind. You have to create and maintain a presence for yourself and your company. Find out where your customers hang out (e.g., trade associations, chambers of commerce, NMSDC events) and show up. The more interactions you have with your current or potential customers, the more you will learn about them, their needs, and their processes. This will speed your sales process as you reassure your customer of your interest in them. If you are able to serve as a volunteer leader in organizations where your customers are able to observe you, you are able to show them your talent, reliability, work ethic, and leadership ability. Active presence definitely has its payoffs!

Some suppliers have the attitude that all they want from the supplier diversity professional is to take them to the decision maker. They do not appreciate that they are already talking to a decision maker. These people view the supplier diversity professionals as gatekeepers. They are! They provide a valued service to the corporations they work for, or they wouldn't survive constant cost-cutting and corporate downsizing. Supplier diversity professionals should be viewed as scouts for the corporations they work for. They are the ones the corporations send out to find qualified new suppliers. Their recommendations mean something. They can carry a message about you to the right people, but only if they trust you and only if you have given them strong talking points about you. You should also know that increasingly, decisions on suppliers are not made by one person but rather by a team of people, oftentimes geographically dispersed around the world. Being a scout is risky: Bring back an MBE that is not prepared and you can't be my scout anymore. Don't bring back any MBEs and what kind of scout are you? An MBE once told me, "Don (one of the best supplier diversity professionals) can't help me!" I responded, "He can. He just hasn't decided to yet." Position yourself in the marketplace to gain insight, build trusting relationships, communicate your value, and show appreciation to your customers. Then repeat the cycle.

Build sustainable, mutually beneficial relationships.

People do business with people they know and trust. So do companies. Give your customers an opportunity to get to know you and like you. In many countries, you may court a potential customer and their family for a year or more, building trust and personal relationships before business is even discussed. In the United States, we think it is all about getting down to business right away. That is a fallacy. It is imperative that you get to know your customers, show them you have their best interests in mind, and demonstrate that you are reliable and can be trusted.

Keep strengthening your relationships with current customers as you pursue new customers. In the midst of Houston's economic crash in the 1980s, HMSDC held an expo where the corporations exhibited to meet new suppliers. I noticed Charles hard at work at the expo. I asked him, "Charles, why are you here? You are already doing business with all of these companies." I'll never forget his response. "Fear," he said, then he explained that Houston's economic crash was causing many businesses to fail. Charles wanted to make sure that all his customers knew that he was alive and well and fully prepared to meet their needs, in each case thanking the corporate member for their business and inquiring what additional needs they might have. Charles was one of the most popular people at that expo!

Strong, mutually beneficial relationships will give you insight into your customer's needs and your opportunities to meet those needs. It will also assure your customer of your sincere interest in serving them.

Listen, then relate.

There's a reason you have two ears and only one mouth: you need to listen twice as much as you talk. If you listen carefully, your customers will tell you exactly what they need and how they do business. They will explain their culture and how they choose suppliers. Armed with that insight, your role is to play back those values and needs, then show how your company meets the criteria and can solve the needs. Adding your thoughts on what's next sets the stage for expanded business and establishes you as a leader. Listen, then relate!

Be persistent.

Years ago, when I asked our corporate members what it took to do business with them, the most common answer was "persistence." I didn't really like the answer. What about better price, better quality, or better service? You mean I have to keep knocking and knocking on your door until you get around to answering it? It didn't seem right from the supplier perspective, but the customer sets the rules. I remember one of our more determined MBEs who deliberately sought out a particular corporate member at two subsequent luncheons and followed up effectively after each, in each case telling what his company did. It wasn't until the third luncheon that the corporate member said, "Good to see you again. I was hoping to see you today. Now what is it that you do?" The MBE was crushed! He wanted to ask, "What do you think we have been talking about for the past six months?" He did not understand the corporate process. Ever since they first met, the corporate member was testing the MBE's true resolve to serve that corporation. Would he follow through on follow-up instructions? Would his persistence continue as evidence of his strong desire to understand the customer and relate to the customer's needs, or was it all about the MBE just getting some business? The corporate member had finally decided that they could rely on and do business with the MBE. Now they are interested in knowing what the MBE did so they could help him fit into the corporate supply chain. I've seen too many businesses fail to understand the process and give up on a prospective customer prematurely, not realizing that they were almost there. Your persistence actually honors the prospective customer and reassures them of your strong desire to understand them and to come through on doing business with them. While today customers are seeking new solutions to their needs and industry leadership from their suppliers, it is still imperative that you be persistent!

Consistently delight your customers!

Andy's highly successful firm had a simple mission statement: "To delight our customers." The goal was not just to meet the terms of the contract, but also to find ways to delight each customer at every opportunity. Show that you are more than reliable. Take a personal interest in delighting your customers. Think of your own shopping experience: In many stores you are left alone to fend for yourself. It's almost impossible to find someone to help you. Then there are the stores (usually doing much more business) where a sales agent meets you at the door, perhaps gives you a refreshment, and asks how they can help you. If you want, they will work with you until you leave (often with an armful of packages). You have a choice in who you do business with. Who do you choose and why? What kind of customer experience are you providing?

Lead! Become the turn-to expert in your industry. Innovate!

Years ago the goal was to get on the bid list. Then you would compete on the basis of price and the lowest bid won. Customers welcomed new suppliers to the bid list to use increased competition to reduce prices. Reverse auctions were used to drive prices even lower, often beyond reason. The buyer-supplier relationship was unhealthy, perhaps abusive.

The market then turned to a more sustainable model where suppliers sought to identify the pressing needs of potential customers, then show how they best could meet those needs. In essence, suppliers were selling solutions instead of products or services. A close relationship between buyer and seller was required to get access to true customer needs and identify the best solution to those needs. Innovation and trust were also factors in building long-term business relationships.

Today, the marketplace demands even more from preferred suppliers. In the past, customers set the required specifications. Today, customers are looking for industry leadership from their suppliers. Customers today expect their suppliers to be experts in their industry and are looking to their suppliers to provide current, innovative ideas and the plan and specs to achieve them. Buyers and suppliers become true partners in their common success and growth.

Grow your capacity to perform.

Most small businesses do not have sufficient capacity to win and perform on contracts with major corporations. Those businesses are forced to drop lower on the supply chain to find opportunities of a size they can compete for. They become invisible to the ultimate customer, making it hard to build their brand and gain access to direct opportunities. An alternate strategy is to form joint ventures or strategic alliances between businesses that can increase your capabilities and your capacity. To be effective in alliances, each business must be seen as a leader in their respective industry, and they have to each bring business to the table. It's been proven that a team of "best in class" firms can outprice and outperform the competition. What are you "best in class" in? Who would complement your skills while opening more doors to opportunity?

It is also at this point that the minority business owner must decide his or her company's future growth strategy. Will it be diversifying the business by acquiring or building complimentary skills? Will it be merging or selling the company to a larger firm? Or will it be acquiring or teaming with other businesses to grow your size and capacity?

Pay it forward!

As you and your company grow, be sure to pay it forward. Invest yourselves in others, and they will continue to invest in you. Donna worked for one of our MBEs, then decided to take that leap of faith and go out on her own. The only problem was that her former employer commanded the market. Donna began her business by positioning herself where she could learn from others. Everything she learned she shared with others through the various organizations in which she was involved. She also was very generous in giving to and serving her community. She frequently sponsored others (including me) in enrichment programs. Much of my success I owe to Donna's example and promotion. Donna became a connector of people to people and people to causes. In the process she developed a large, unpaid referral base for her company. When someone mentioned her industry, the first thought was Donna. Additionally, Donna positioned herself to identify and capitalize on emerging trends where she could differentiate her company from her competitors. Thus, Donna was the first in her industry to embrace the quality movement in the 1980s and achieve ISO 9000 certification. As her industry tanked, she used her contacts to better understand emerging customer needs, then she literally transformed her company around innovative strategies to fulfill those needs. Today, Donna is one of America's leading and most respected business owners. Her example shows that when you give, you get—not just a good feeling inside from helping others, but also strong relationships that fuel your success.

In summary, you can't rest on your laurels. The marketplace is moving too fast for you to sit still even for a moment. Successful MBEs must constantly look for emerging opportunities, marketplace trends, and developments and be ready to capitalize on them with innovative solutions. You are known not so much for all you have accomplished in the past, but for the value you are capable of delivering to your customers today and into the future.

4
Words of Wisdom from Minority Business Owners

"You must have a product or service that you truly believe in and that you are really good at. You must be proud of that product or service and be absolutely crazy about providing the very best delivery of that product and service. At the end of the day, you may get in because you are an MBE, but they will only keep you because of the service and the quality of the product that you provide. The only way to stay in is to be amazing at what you do."

—*Provider of construction services, located in Indiana*

"It's important to be consistent, to be self-motivated and driven. Push yourself and be hard on yourself to perform. Have a positive outlook, educate yourself every day, master your craft, and connect with others who are in your field."

—*Clothing recycler*

"Always ask others what they do. Ask where they get their clients. Find ways to help them or introduce them to someone that can help them. I believe in karma. It always come back."

—*Field services company, providing property repair services for foreclosed properties*

"MBEs really need to look at the value they bring. What differentiates you? You must look outside the box. Look at what's going to provide sustainability. Just providing service is not enough. You must be an asset. You must be a partner to your client, do more than providing service, and take ownership of the responsibility."

—*Engineering firm, located in Pennsylvania*

"Get involved. Attend as many local, regional and national events that you can. Participate in networking events. There are many opportunities that will allow you to have dialogue with the various organizations that you're trying to do business with. Never, ever stop moving. Keep going. The more people you know the better off you will be."

—*CEO of a company that provides procurement services, located in Louisiana*

"MBEs should be flexible with their vision. Many MBEs see themselves being in whatever business they choose as opposed to seeing themselves as entrepreneurs open to different ways to grow a business. Flexibility is what your business is and can be. If you look at major firms, they are not just doing one thing. They may grow in one area; however, they are doing multiple things. Broaden the opportunities that you are open to. You can't do everything, but you can listen to ideas that might be outside of what you originally planned. If you have such a narrow focus and refuse to go outside of that focus, you may be abandoning the opportunity to build a truly successful minority-owned business."

—*Owner of a CPA firm, located in Houston, Texas*

"Follow your passion. It doesn't really matter what business you're in, but you must follow your passion and be really good at it."

—*Supplier diversity professional, located in Louisiana*

"Be very honest with yourself about what you don't know and find the team members to fill in gaps. Finding people to compliment you and your team is very important and key. In the beginning when you're small and by yourself, you have to rely on yourself because that's all you have. As you start to grow, you need to have a strong team. The ability to know your weakness and finding key people is an important trait for success."

—*One of the largest staffing firms in the country, located in New York*

"Tenacity is critical, and demonstrated ability is important to get you over the walls."

— *Supplier diversity professional, located in Houston, Texas*

"First, for any company to be successful, they need to really know and understand their market and their target audience. They have to know how they fit in their industry. To give you an example, take a logistics company. Companies are now using more heavy-haul type of companies. They are not using box trucks. So MBEs shouldn't spend their time trying to get into a corporation when it does not look like it's a good fit. It's truly about knowing your market and knowing your competition. For a diverse business to be successful, they have to really understand the market. Understand who it is that you're trying to do business with and how they do business, even if it's just trying to schedule meetings to do fact finding."

—*Supplier diversity manager in the construction of oil and gas facilities*

Some Top Tips for MBEs:

- Be authentic.
- Be humble.
- Be patient.
- Establish yourself.
- Show commitment to your business.
- Research and know the company you are pursuing.
- Prioritize customer service. Do the little things that make the difference.
- Work with other minority groups, not just your minority group.

—*Former president of a local Asian chamber of commerce*

"Sometimes running a minority-owned company is like driving in New York traffic. It's scary, overwhelming, adventurous. There is so much to be aware of and keep your eyes on: cyclists, food vendors, rude taxi drivers, Ubers, everyone rushing to get somewhere, obstacles, stress, loud impatient horns blaring, pushing and shoving, rude 'get-out-of-my-way' people, challenges, excitement. You must stay alert, but there are so many distractions lights, tall buildings, and lots of people all vying for your attention. If you are to reach your desired destination safely, you must stay focused and alert. It's very similar to building a successful minority-owned company, because sometimes there are many, many distractions. If you are going to succeed, you must train yourself to stay focused and alert at all times."

—*Author Ed Ryland*

5
MBEs: Strong as the Golden Gate Bridge

Recently I attended a meeting in San Francisco with some of the most successful minority-owned businesses across the country. We were there along with presidents of minority business organizations and leaders of corporations, some of the most dedicated and knowledgeable individuals around diversity and minority business. While there I took a walk across the Golden Gate Bridge, an iconic structure. Just to experience the magnitude of this amazing architecture, I could not resist thinking about the history behind the bridge. While watching hundreds all around me looking with amazement at the views around the bridge, I wondered what attracted them to the bridge. Why such interest and significance? Looking around as far as I could see, I witnessed a very diverse, economically strong community that is rich in culture. While walking across, I was reminded of what it took to build such a magnificent structure—the intricate details, strength, engineering, and integrity. It took from 1933 to 1937, four years which represented vision, commitment, dedication, persistence, and hard work. Many years later, the bridge is still standing strong. As I looked across the city, you could see how populated and diverse it was. Just to think that in 1906, this city was virtually wiped out by an earthquake that almost completely destroyed it, and now it's one of the most vibrant economic cities in the country. At the core of that rebuilding and the core of the economic strength is the minority business community. You could see it all around you: Asians, Japanese, Hispanics, African Americans. You could see that this city demonstrates the value of minority-owned businesses and what a successful minority-owned business looks like. These are the characteristics you would need to build a strong minority-owned business. If you remove the minority businesses from this city, the city would no longer exist. That's what minority-owned companies do for our country, our cities, and our communities.

These are the same characteristics you need to build a sustainable, successful minority-owned business. If you find yourself in a situation where you need to rebuild, know that you can. Even if you have been wiped out completely, stick to your core values, learn from your mistakes, ask for help, look for new and innovative resources, recommit yourself, roll up your sleeves, go to work, and watch your unbelievable rebound!

While in San Francisco I also had a lunch conversation with a group of minority-owned businesses and leaders involved with minority business development. We started the conversation with just casual talk about the world, and then the conversation turned to what makes a successful minority-owned business. Here are some of the comments:

"Don't think of yourself as a minority and that there are some barriers you will have to overcome. Overcoming those barriers should not be your objective; your objective should be, what do I need to deliver quality service and who am I? Look at yourself and ask, why do I want my own business?"

—*Provider of industrial building supplies.*

"You must be quality driven and value added. How can you add value? I never care about the money; the money is a byproduct of the work I do and the reputation that I have. The quality of work that you continue to deliver will produce the money. Culture is important, [meaning] how you engage with your customers and potential customers. You do not want to nickel and dime them. Go the extra step—don't think about how much money you will get from a particular client, but think about what kind of recommendation they will give. It's the way you think and the way you do things that will make a difference. There is no price that you can put on a great recommendation. If I do a bad job, I cannot go back. With a recommendation, you have someone in your corner that can say here's what and how I've done it and here's what I can do."

—*Owner of a business intelligence and data warehousing business, located in Florida*

"Within your service offering, be prepared to show that you are the best so that a supplier diversity person can advocate for you once you get into an organization. You must perform without a lot of problems. The best companies that I have seen do this well, whether first- or second-tier, are the ones we don't hear anything about once they get in. That means to the company that you are doing a good job for the specific department and that the manager is satisfied with the work that you are doing. When we don't hear about any issues, that means you have your head down and you are taking care of business. You have identified what our needs are, and you are delivering on those needs and building on those needs as well. You are also in collaboration with the specific department and the department manager looking for other needs where you can position yourself to expand into."

—*Supplier diversity professional*

6

A Lesson on Humility—A Key Component of Success

True humility is a key component of success. I learned that the hard way. It began when I started to make some moves in the community and the real estate world. I was the first African American to be elected to the Houston Association of Realtors board, and I was considered one of the most impactful minority real estate professionals in Houston, Texas. I had served in various capacities and was considered a "go-to" thought leader when it came to real estate and real estate issues. I finally had made it in a majority world.

I started working hard in the Houston Association of Realtors organization, tirelessly chairing committees, working on special projects, and being a spokesperson. Finally, I was elected to be a part of the exclusive executive team. Man, I really had made it now! Now I was truly a success. I was accepted not just by the minority community, but by the majority community and not just a majority community, but the largest real estate organization in the country.

I ascended to the vice chair position. Traditionally, that meant I would go on to become the chair of this great organization. Before that happened, I began to hear rumors. A very good friend of mine called me and said, "Hey, let's have lunch." He began to share with me the historical politics of the organization. He said, "Hey man, they don't want you to become chair of this organization, and they are planning to do everything they can to stop you."

At that point I was successful, perhaps too vocal and too impactful. This was a point in my life where I was confident and very close to cocky. I thought I had humility, but really I didn't have a clue about what real humility was. Another close friend told me, "When you lose it, you find it." I will never forget that conversation. This is an important point that I want you to get: don't underestimate my friend's comment. When you start losing things that are important to you—careers, family members, possessions, your health—you get a true sense of your humility. So, recognizing that what I was hearing was true, I put on the most aggressive strategic campaign that I had ever done in my life. You would have thought I was running for president of the United States. I'm smiling now just thinking about it, but there were no smiles back then. I enlisted my entire family and friends who were secretly working behind the scenes to make sure that we sent a strong message whether I won or lost.

We began meeting with people, telling them about my platform and why I should be the next chair. We were getting commitments for support and sending out information on my behalf, letting the powers that be know that we were not just going to sit here and do nothing. My entire life was built around standing up for what you believe and fighting, win, lose, or draw. My mother came down from St Louis. This was the time of the fax machine, but she had never used one before. It's funny thinking about that now. She put on her glasses, sat down at the fax machine, and began punching numbers very, very, very slowly. It probably took her five minutes to punch in one number, but what a joy. My wife was involved and really pissed that her husband was being treated in such a way, yet happy and supportive that we were fighting back. We began sending packages of information by overnight special delivery, explaining why I should be the next chair of the organization. It was a great campaign full of energy and excitement. It's funny what passion, focus, and purpose can achieve. As a minority business owner this is what you will need.

I was able to successfully assist getting other minorities elected to the board, and I thought that they would be my strongest supporters. Here's another lesson for you: don't assume just because they look like you and talk to you that they are really your supporters. This goes for anyone. We have to be careful of that "crab in the bucket" syndrome. It was alive and well a hundred years ago, and it's alive and well today. The big day came. I practiced my speech, polishing it over and over and over again. I prayed day and night, asking, "God, whatever happens, just let me accept it."

We got down to the votes. All the votes were cast and the outcome was announced—the votes were tied. Tied? Really? From the look on the face of the person overseeing the votes, no one really believed that we were tied. By that time, it had become apparent that those involved in the process had developed a reputation of shady and unethical behavior. Since we were tied, the person overseeing the elections quickly said, "Well, let's do it by lot. We'll just pick one of the two names from a jar. Whoever's name we pick will be the chair." He then commenced to pulling a name but never shared the paper pulled with the board. Just like that they announced that my opponent was the winner. I sat there very composed looking around the room. I finally knew what true humility was like. I had risen to the top of my game, and now how was I going to face the community, my family, and everybody who supported me with this news?

This is what I did, and why. It does not matter what's going on in your life, successes or failures. God will and can step in at any time. He will help you deliver the news, and he will help you get the glory out of any situation. So I thanked everybody, shook everyone's hand, and went to the driving range at the golf course and began to pray, asking God to help me remove the anger, the resentment, and the homicidal thoughts I had. With all I've given to this organization and all that I've done in my business, how could they? While I was on the golf course, one of my good friends, councilman Judson Robinson, called me to check on the results since he was also involved in supporting me early in my career. I shared the news with him and he said, "Vengeance is mine says the Lord." I didn't quite know what he meant when he said it, but now I do. For about four years, I prayed daily to have God remove the resentment and anger that I had against the people and the organization. You know when you pray and forgive others, you get the benefit. And that's exactly what began to happen to me. Not only did I better understand humility, I began to appreciate, respect, and work on true humility.

I pressed on and that very same organization, at my insistence, created the Institute for Diversity and Inclusion. It was the first time an internal entity like that was created. Fast forward to where I am now, and most of those who plotted against me are no longer in this business. The minorities who did not support me no longer have their own firms but are now working for other folks and have very limited exposure in this industry. I have gone on to build one of the most successful minority-owned commercial real estate firms in the country. So what's the message here? Work hard, play hard, stay involved. Most of all, monitor your humility and keep an open mind. You can't assume who will or won't support you. And by the way, the vast majority of folks on that board supported me and we remain friends today. Humility is a key component to minority business success.

Here's what I know: If I had achieved what I thought I wanted, I would be out of business today, no question in my mind. Instead, I've gone on to be the cofounder of the first national minority-owned commercial real estate firm in the country, and I have received numerous awards and recognitions from my peers and from the most prestigious real estate organizations in the country. Most recently, I received the Lifetime Achievement Award from Houston CoreNet, a part of CoreNet Global, which is the most recognized corporate real estate organization in the country.

7
Wise Counsel from a Strong Leader

I had a very rich conversation with a president of one of the largest regional minority supplier development organizations. They had more than twenty-five years of seeing minority-owned businesses starting to grow, and unfortunately some go out of business. Here are their words of wisdom. Read carefully so you don't become a part of the gone-out-of-business group.

>There are so many things to consider based on where you are. If you are a new minority-owned business or small minority-owned business I cannot talk enough about networking and relationships. Relationships are the foundation. However, those that you're trying to build relationships with don't want any more relationships. Larger minority-owned businesses would be far more successful if not for their aggressive or pushy approach. People need to perceive you as a good person, particularly during this politically sensitive environment where the perception is they don't have to take minority-owned business as seriously. Honesty and integrity are key. You must figure out what your client wants and do it. Know what you can deliver and what you cannot. One of the hardest things to do is to turn away business; every business is not good business. Understand exactly what you can do. Also take care of your talent. Treat them right. It is very hard to find good talent. In some ways, it's harder now for MBEs than it was twenty years ago, particularly for the private sector and private sector inclusion. Now, minority-owned businesses are just one more group of several minority disadvantage groups. If I have to talk about the top three things I would advise minority-owned companies to do, it would be first focus on

relationships and serious conversations where they say, "Let me see what you got and see if there is an opportunity for you." Be persistent but not a pest. Constantly communicate. Relationships are personal, and sometimes we forget that it is just another person we are communicating with. Have small conversations where the person does not have to stress or be on their guard. Relationships may not always start with the person you want to do business with, but they may be the very person that has the right connection for you. Decision makers have very limited resources. They want to know how you will help them make their job easier. So ask the question, "What do you think it would take to make your job easier?" Second, focus on technology. How can technology make your business easier? Be technologically efficient and driven, and find a technology solution. Third, good talent is crucial. It may not be staff. It may be collaborating with partners. This could be a game changer. Also don't just stay in your lane, align yourself with organizations that are specific to your field. You need to know where you can stretch because you can't do everything. Sell what you can really deliver. And finally, I believe minority-owned businesses are at risk when it comes to their cash flow and back-end operations. These are issues that cause some of the best firms to go out of business.

—*President of one of the largest minority supplier development councils*

"The fact that you're in business means that you are capable. That's one of the biggest hurdles. Large firms are wired to think that you don't perform. How do you get a seat at the table? That's when agencies like the National Minority Supplier Development Council and the National Minority Business Development Agency can be valuable. You need to recognize that you can't do everything for everyone. You need to know clearly who you are interfacing with in the procurement environment that will help you get business."

—*Nuclear solutions business, located in North Carolina*

"Work hard and identify opportunities. You should get involved in something that you know. It helps to better minimize the risk if you have knowledge of what you do. Knowing your industry is key."

—*Office supply business, located in South Africa*

"Trust. Clients are putting their goods in your hand. You must have a good tracking and on-time delivery systems so that goods are not damaged or stolen. There is a lot of hijacking in South Africa, so you must know how to handle unique situations."

—*Logistics company with twenty-four years in the business, located in South Africa*

"Determination and after service sale support is very important."

—*Air conditioning business located in South Africa*

"A good, sustainable minority-owned business is being prepared for the opportunity, making sure you have the knowledge and the experience, and also having people that can help you build it quickly. You must have relationships with people who believe in you. Before you can sell anything, people have to believe in you and you have to be confident that you can deliver. Additionally, you need an advisor, someone who will give you the good, bad, and ugly about what you have and what you don't have. They will focus on how to build you up and how to move you forward. With these elements, a little prayer and being in the right place at the right time, while also getting a break, will contribute to your success. When you think about those who have been successful, there is someone that came along and gave them an opportunity and put them in a place that they did not see coming. One of the main things that gave me the confidence that I could be successful was my parents. My parents bought a two-hundred-acre farm. I now realize that you cannot be more of an entrepreneur than being a farmer. Working with them and understanding what they did year after year helped me to understand and focus on what you want, and that what you need to do takes focus dedication and hard work. Ask lots of questions, keep your eyes open, and have an open mind. Your business should evolve to where there is a need and an opportunity. Just because you start in one area or field does not mean you have to stay there forever. Also consider public speaking, as this has helped my business."

—*Cyber security and system supports company, located in Cincinnati, Ohio*

"As a former Vietnam vet, I learn to fight, focus, and win. You must have a gift of discernment. Discernment gives you that 'it' factor, where people are attracted to you. You can walk in a room, and certain people will look at you and want to talk to you. Discernment gives you the ability to be proactive and have selective hearing where you only hear the good part. You let the bad part in one ear and out the other. Technology has taken us extremely fast into this new era of business, so be prepared to move fast, stay in shape, and make sure you have good health. There is a new word being used. 'Pivoting' means a quick turnaround. There's no time to think. It becomes natural. The formula for success is when you have skills to find the need that people have. This will lead to success."

—*President and founder of the General Motors Minority Dealers Association and one of the founders of the National Minority Auto Dealership Association*

"First, you must identify strengths and weaknesses. Really search for the internal aspect of your willingness to sacrifice the time and subscribe to change."

—*Consultant who works with MBEs to grow them and provide private equity, located in Chicago, Illinois*

"The starting point is to identify organizations like the National Minority Supplier Development Council. These organizations have opportunities to do a SWOT (strengths, weakness, opportunities, and threats) analysis on your company."

—*IT architect, located in Chicago, Illinois*

8
From the Eleventh Floor to the Lobby

Recently I was in New York for a business conference. As you know in New York, it's all hustle and bustle, hurry up, hurry up, and many people moving back and forth from all over the world. While on my way down from my room, which was on the eleventh floor, more hotel guests began to enter the elevator to ride down. Typically, most of us when we get on an elevator either nod or don't say anything at all. Very rarely do we engage the people on the elevator in a conversation that will allow us to (1) understand what they do or (2) share with them what we do. In this particular situation, I didn't feel like engaging in conversation.

There was a young person on the elevator who looked like she was a student and really didn't have much to add to what I was trying to accomplish. Well, when I reached the fifth floor, I decided to turn around and say, "Hey how are you? Where are you from?" She went on to say she was from Florida.

I said, "Oh ok, oh really!?" I asked, "You left the warm weather to come here to this cold wet city?"

"Yeah," she said, "and I'm dreading it."

"Well what do you do?" I asked.

"I'm in television," she replied.

By that time, we had hit the lobby floor. I thought to myself, what a wasted opportunity that I had just had. I'm sure many of you have experienced the same thing. Had I started that conversation on the eleventh floor, by the time I reached the lobby I would have engaged this young lady in a conversation that would have led me to ask more questions about what she did in the television world and how I could connect with her for future projects that I'm working on. Here's the lesson: never waste an opportunity to network and talk to others about what they do and what you do. Second, never underestimate a person's worth by what you assume they are based on their looks. She/he's too young, She/he's too short, she/he doesn't look like they have an important job . . . well I may have just missed a tremendous opportunity from the eleventh floor to the lobby.

—*Author Ed Ryland*

"It takes persistence, a plan, integrity, and sticking to that plan. You must leverage what you don't know. Be okay with that, and utilize other people to offset what you don't know."

—*Security service company, located in Los Angeles, California*

"First, your company must have the right value proposition. This is key. Second, you must have the right team to offer excellent services. After you have accomplished this, utilize organizations that work to grow your business and build relationships that leads to access. This will allow you to compete with MBEs and non-MBE companies and give you a competitive edge."

—*Owner of a holding company located in Cincinnati, Ohio, that acquires other companies*

"It has nothing to do with being minority. Everything must be intentional. You must create a culture of excellence. We believe in empowering our staff. If you treat your staff well, they will treat your clients well."

—*Owner of a warehouse and distribution company, located in Chicago, Illinois*

"MBEs must be compliant. You cannot expect to win business if you're not qualified. Your books and certifications must be kept current at all times—not just your MBE certifications but professional certifications as well. Your company must be able to withstand an audit. You need to be proactive and go after the business. Don't think just because you are an MBE that the business is going to come to you or that companies have to do business with you. You must win the business on your own merit. An MBE should be a value-add, not for themselves but for their customers. You must be sustainable and have capacity. Companies do not want you to get ready after the fact, they want you to be ready when you knock on the door. That means having a line of credit and being realistic about your capacities. Clients don't want you calling them every week for your money. You must use technology and data analytics. Investing in tools that are used in your industry will help you find the needle in the haystack. That's what the large competitor companies are doing. Finally, practice your elevator pitch to perfection."

—*Owner of a database company for government contracting, located in Washington, DC*

"MBEs should focus on networking and adding value. Your value-add should be at least ten times your cost. Continue to think about creating value."

—*Owner of a minority supplier database organization, located in Houston, Texas*

"One of the most important things for a minority-owned business or any business is for a salesperson to think in terms of relationships versus transactions. Relationships are built in thousands of interactions over time—thousands of interactions with you and the company or the person. One bad interaction can set the relationship back: one person being rude, one person being disrespectful, one terrible billing mishap. Each interaction impacts the relationship and that transfers over to the brand. Those things impact the perception of your company and the brand of your company. Brand isn't just what you put on your website or brochure, it's every interaction someone has with you and your company. As the key business or marketing person, your job is to put forth the brand, making sure everything you are projecting is how you are positioning your brand. Ultimately the brand is not what you see it is, it's what other people perceive it to be. Minority businesses, like any businesses, can fall into the trap of racing to the bottom, where only one company gets to be the cheapest. It is not a great business decision to be the cheapest because the only thing someone else has to do is to offer a lower price, and now they are the cheapest. It is not a sustainable business to be the least expensive. You must work harder than that. Know who you are; many firms cannot tell you who they are. They will say we do this, this, and this, but who are you when no one is looking? Who are you without even trying? What do you deliver on without even thinking twice about it? That's where you start with a sustainable position because you know you can deliver. Be a storyteller. Be able to tell who you are and what you do in a way that carries people with you, and that excites people as much as it excites you telling it. Tell the idea behind the company, how they did it, and why they did it. "Why" is really an interesting question. People remember stories, engaging stories. Lean into the future. One of the hardest things—and it's really easy to not do—is to lean into the future. One way to do that is by hiring young people because they know different things. They will push you, and they lean into technology. Find your community. Don't be the smartest person in the room. Find the place where you can get resources and support wherever you need. It is hard to do it by yourself, but find a way to share your talent and give back."

—*Owner of a marketing and consulting firm, located in California*

"It's important that MBEs prove their capability and ability for capacity. Explain how you can work for large firms even though you may be a one- or five-person operation. Advertising is also important. You may not be able to hire an ad agency, but it is important that your brochures, capability statements, and all of your material have the same message. The appearance is very important. When you're working with larger firms, you're working with executives, and you should appear larger than you are."

—Provider of state and local tax advisory services, located in Dallas, Texas

"MBE should enhance their elevator pitch, understand their capability, and be able to share that. Identify customers that can grow their business in their core competency. Collaborate with other MBEs. Develop your business strategies responsibly with sound financial backing."

—Owner of an industrial facilities management and waste management firm, located in Detroit, Michigan

"Leverage your successes and use them to propel yourself. The momentum is important to push you forward. When you meet people, stay in touch constantly. This is a 24-7 world, so it is important to stay in front of customers and future customers constantly. Finally, nothing beats talent. Make sure you have the right team to help you grow and scale."

—Operator of a data analytics solutions firm, located in Pasadena, California

"Any business in a start-up mode should address three critical elements. First is fear. Don't be afraid to move forward and make contacts. The second issue is that many MBEs do not reach out to other resources to get additional information about things they don't know. Third is financials. While financials are a major concern, if you put the right pieces in place, the financials will come. There are so many elements to running a small business and building a successful business. Don't take anything for granted, and get a mentor."

—Owner of a specialty environmental cleaning firm, located in Arizona

"Focus first on being in a successful business. Know the business you're in and what you are skilled at doing. There was a report put out that explains how peoples' work is shaped by why they work. There are three factors that increase motivation and three factors that bring down our motivation. If your work is something you enjoy, it becomes like play because one of the reasons you work is that you enjoy your work. When motivation is high, productivity is high. If you have a purpose, motivation is high. If you have the potential to do something else, motivation is high. If you are working to deal with emotional pressures or economic pressures, wanting to deal with the inertia of all these things will bring your motivation down. The other thing MBEs need to do is ask more questions. We oftentimes think our job is to tell people more about what we do. Well, no one is really interested in that. Seventy percent of decision-makers are making decisions based upon their need. You have to understand what their need is and ask questions that let them know you are interested in solving their problem. There are times we will face discrimination and racism. That's a fact of life. It is a human condition that all people have biases, but once you look at the question of how racism or bias affect you, ask, 'What can I do better?' One side of the equation is who's going to lock the door because of my race or gender. The other side is what you can do to improve yourself and your business so that you make yourself as strong as you can be. If you sit around constantly saying there are barriers that you can't get through, you will have defeated yourself already. There is lots of research that proves teams that are diverse and collaborative outperform more talented teams. A word about competition: our job is not to always be competing against each other. Sometimes iron sharpens iron, and we need each other. It's important to start building more strategic alliances."

—*Management consulting firm focused on diverse and inclusive workplaces, located in Cincinnati, Ohio*

"MBEs have to be good listeners. Oftentimes MBEs tell you what they do, but very few times do they ask what is it you need. The successful MBEs will listen and will apply those services, or they will change their current offerings to meet the needs of the client. Nothing is more rewarding than to have an MBE fix an issue for our sourcing and procurement team. That's when you become a true partner. From there, those relationships will build, and we can add more things to your portfolio. So if you fix that problem, you can fix this problem. Now you become a true partner, if you can get into strategic conversations that lead to saying, 'How can I help you with your business?' as opposed to, 'Do you buy this?' You will meet with a higher degree of success and longevity by fixing our business issues. So you need to be a fixer. You need to have a solution to fix the issue."

—*Supplier diversity professional, located in Houston, Texas*

"Know what your market strategy and cash strategy are and what they will be. You need to have a good understanding of what your market is, how you will work in that market, and how you will support that market strategy from a cash position. You may get the business, but if it is not supported from a market perspective, you will not be successful."

—*Owner of a recruiting and staffing firm located in Brentwood, Tennessee*

"You must be persistent, consistent, and dedicated to your craft. Focus on building relationships and be consistent with that effort. Be open to what others have to offer. Don't give up, but don't be a pest."

—*Former supplier diversity professional and currently an MBE with a national janitorial service company, located in Houston, Texas*

"Have a product or service that is in demand. Dedicate yourself to that product or service, and be the best at it. One of the mistakes many businesses fall into is the trap of trying to be everything to everybody. Know your strength, and know as a small business that you only get one shot to make a mistake. That mistake can cost you your business. Know your lane, get all the training you can, and be the best at it. In terms of growth, most of us start out as subcontractors to larger primes. While that is great, the mistake is getting too comfortable with only being a subcontractor and not looking to grow capacity. You must look for ways to be a prime contractor. MBEs should be mindful of taking what's left from the primes. This is not a negative thing, but you don't grow capacity that way. You can make money that way, you can make a living that way, but you have to look for ways to grow your capacity to be a prime. Look for ways to joint venture, and look at subcontracting as a way to audition to perform for that client. Ask the client what they need to see from your firm in order for you to compete as a prime. See yourself emerging into a prime. Show that you can perform as a prime and that you are stable, you are trustworthy, and you have a good product or service. If you are providing a quality service or product, there is enough room for you to be a prime. But you have to be bold enough to do it. You will not reach your maximum potential staying in a subcontractor's role. Be careful not to put all your chips in one bowl."

—*Owner of a project management and consulting services firm, located in Houston, Texas*

"You must have a strong back office, strong administrative support, and strong finances. If you want to grow from a one- or two-person office to something larger, you must know how to delegate. Delegate away those things you are not so good at, and pay them well to do it."

—*Employee at a Minority Business Development Agency (MBDA) center*

"It takes hard work, integrity, honesty, and persistence. Always do the right thing, and success will come to you. You must really work hard to get where you want to be."

—*Builder of electrical control panels for the oil and gas industry, located in Houston, Texas*

"Number one, be a successful business owner. Being a successful minority business owner will follow. There is no handbook or *Business Ownership for Dummies* available which could teach you everything you need to know to be a successful business owner. My recommendation is to surround yourself with six business owners you honor and respect, each one with a different expertise: strategy, sales, innovation, technology, finance, and growth/scaling. Be around these experts as your circle of friends. Their lessons learned will become your lessons learned! Success will follow, and in turn you will be a successful business enterprise, which happens to be minority."

—*Safety solutions consultant, located in California*

"Number one is resilience because out here as a minority owned firm, you have to understand the reality of the world. We may want to think that all we have to do is be the best at whatever we do, and companies are going to come and they will buy it. That's not true. We have to be the best at what we're going to produce, but also understand that there are a number of people who are still not going to come your way, no matter how good you are, and they will have a variety of reasons for that. If you get turned off and you get disenchanted because you're not moving along as fast as you think, then eventually you are going to give up. So you have to have the resilience and match that with confidence in your ability to say, 'Okay, I'm in here for the long haul. I know that I'm good at what I do. I just have to find the right kind of market and the right people to work with me and to use my services.' So it takes resilience and competence. I'm saying that just as my personal testimony, because

I sit here some days going, 'You know, there's a guy out there who can barely spell his name making two million dollars. Why!?'"

—*Provider of e-learning and multimedia communications, located in Hamden, Connecticut*

9
Nine Key Tips for MBE Success

Here are some things for you to think about as you are building your successful minority-owned business.

Be organized.

I do this through a daily prioritized list, ensuring that the most important business issues get addressed and that I don't waste valuable time on what is not the "highest and best" use of my time.

Document everything.

Keeping detailed records is just smart business. Your memory really isn't as great as you think it is for minor details, especially if you need to defend a financial or legal position. Document and safeguard. You will be glad you did.

Know your competition.

Do not fear competition. Look at it as a way to distinguish your value proposition. Benchmark and learn from their successes and failures.

Really understand your risk.

I like to approach most business decisions by asking, "What is the exit strategy? What is the worst-case business and financial scenario?" By doing this I can get a better, more realistic understanding of the potential rewards. Here you should engage a CPA and legal team before committing to any significant decision.

Innovate and create.

We hear and talk a lot about being innovative and creative. But are we really? When was the last time you thought about doing something that was really innovative and creative? What was your thought process? How did you start? What problem did you solve? What excitement did you bring to your client or to the marketplace? In order to be innovative and creative, you have to think wild and crazy. You cannot worry about what others may think. Let yourself dream the impossible. Go somewhere different, get around different people, and open your mind and imagination. Something will come. Then you will stand out from the competition.

Don't get scattered.

Not every opportunity is the right opportunity. Stay focused. There will be many things fighting for your attention. Consistent patience will ensure that the right resources are directed to the right business development and service delivery opportunity. Be careful not to let setbacks take you off of the big picture and your goal.

Know that there's no gain without pain.

You must be willing to make sacrifices in your personal, family, and business life. There may be less meat in those beans for a while. Early to rise, late to sleep. In the long run it will all pay off.

Create raving fans.

Now that you have the business, how do you ensure that you keep it and have existing clients help grow your business? You do it through exceptional customer service. The client may not always be right, but they should feel like they selected the right firm for their product or service. If you think you are doing a great job, do more. Spot a problem before they do. Great customer service is the lifeblood of your business.

Repeat, then repeat again.

Repeating successful behavior and strategies is a key component to making money in business. You have to do what's necessary daily to be successful long term. Repeat it until it becomes second nature or stops working. This will create positive, long-term habits that will help your business be sustainable and make money in the long run.

—*Author Ed Ryland*

10
Iconic MBEs

Some time ago, I read a book on iconic minority entrepreneurs. I was very curious as to what made them the Supermen and Superwomen they were. What was the makeup of these highly successful minority business owners, who ran some of the largest companies in the country? These iconic MBEs have developed their individual road maps to success. I call their road maps masterpieces because if you look at the details of their art (that is, the art of minority business development), you will find intricate details. And like a masterpiece, their businesses are crafted with extraordinary skill, representing a supreme intellectual achievement, their greatest piece of work. These MBEs embody that definition. They have taken the time and the diligence to sculpt, mold, and develop a product or service that only Leonardo da Vinci could rival. Their masterpieces are the backgrounds they have laid their businesses out on, the canvases they have chosen to build their stories on, the colors and designs they have chosen, the inspirations behind the designs, and the sacrifices they have made. Below are few of these heroic minority business owners and their reflections on their careers. Enjoy their stories, and let their journeys inspire you to join this list of iconic MBEs.

There is a quote from **A. G. Gaston** that says money has no color. If you can build a better mousetrap, it won't matter whether you are black or white. People will buy it. Mr. Gaston was named Black Enterprise Entrepreneur of the Century in 1992 at the age of 100. He built a complex of companies in Birmingham, Alabama, during a time when it was considered the most segregated city in America. He launched the Booker T. Washington Insurance Company in 1932 and Citizens Federal Savings Bank in 1957 to serve black consumers ignored by white institutions.

What gave **Robert L. Johnson** the crazy idea that he could possibly start a network addressing the needs of black audiences and become a multimillionaire? It's stupid! I'm sure you have heard similar comments about thoughts and aspirations you may have had. But here's the difference: Johnson did not listen to the negative talk. He stayed focused on his passion, his vision, and his desire to change the world, and look at him today. Johnson, is the founder of BET, a black entertainment television cable network. Johnson's comment on networking is that all business is personal. Make your friends before you need them. One of his quotes is, "We look for strategic partners that can bring something to the equation. I believe that two plus two should equal five."

I can remember thinking deeply about **Russell Simmons,** the hiphopreneur, founder of Def Jam Recordings and founder of Rush Communications and affiliate companies. He sums up his approach to business when he advises to be patient and learn everything you can about the business that you're entering. Hire people who are smarter than you. Find "rabbis" to teach you what you need to know.

Come on, really? A kinky-haired black woman with all the stereotypical looks that America has bestowed upon us is going to open up a business? No freaking way. Well, she did. **Emma C. Chappell** was a divorced mom who started a banking and financial services firm. She states nothing in the world can take the place of persistence. Above all else, entrepreneurs must have clarity. They must clearly define the company's mission, products, services, and strategy. "Leadership can only be demonstrated through example. I never asked someone to do something that I wouldn't do or haven't done," Chappell once said. Just think about what it took to be a minority woman with enough guts and audacity to start a lending institution in a country where minorities could not even get a loan to start a business. That is amazing.

What are you listening to? Who are you letting get in your head about your abilities and limitations, what you can or cannot do? Is it family members and friends? Or is it so-called supporters and undercover haters? Are you letting critics take up free space in your head? If you are, I would give an eviction notice immediately! Listen to the wisdom of **Mel Farr,** owner of Mel Farr Automotive Group, Inc., a new and used domestic and foreign automobile company. Farr speaks of the "winner's mentality." Winners visualize future success, cause change, focus on customers, continually improve, and hang with other winners. As Farr said, they are "often pleased but never satisfied."

It's not what happened to these iconic entrepreneurs. It's their attitudes about what happened to them. If they get knocked, down their attitude is, "I can get back up." That should be your attitude. If they are praised and have huge success, they accept gracefully and humbly. They keep looking for ways to be even better, always grateful and always looking for ways to improve. Take for example **Johnson H. Johnson,** founder of the Johnson Publishing Company. Johnson's tip for success is that the most important thing a manager can learn is the ability to analyze a situation quickly and think his or her way out of it. One of his quotes is, "I run scared every business day and use every legal means necessary to survive and grow." Johnson's companies included a magazine, beauty supply companies, and a publishing organization.

As I began to concentrate and really absorb the magnitude of these tremendous, courageous, faithful, and talented iconic entrepreneurs, I can't help but think about my own journey and some of the tools that I have implemented in my personal and business life that mirror some of the things they have done. I have found myself taking inspiration from their passion, successes, and energy to fuel me when things are challenging. When I find myself on the seesaw of entrepreneurship, I'm reminded of the comments from **Herman J. Russell,** founder of H. J. Russell and Company, a construction, property management, real estate development, and airport concessions company. Russell lived by being true to himself, being punctual, and mastering the art of saving a dollar. He said, "How I operated in my life was how I ran my company. I budgeted for everything. I didn't leave anything to chance." What did he mean? For me this means don't spend more than you make, make as much as you can, save as much as you can, and give as much as you can.

I remember their stories and their challenges every time I think about how life has been for me. I remember them each time I think about losing an account, asking what I could have done differently and what I could have done better. I remember them each time I think about being asked to participate in a career-breaking assignment and what I did to deserve it.

This is the type of minority entrepreneurship that drives you to never want to stop—that keeps you focused, that keeps telling you they have done it so you can do it to.

Do these iconic minority entrepreneurs have something that you don't have or something that you can never get? I don't think so. How bad do you want it?

11
More Words of Wisdom from Minority Business Owners

"First, MBEs needs to understand what they would do to help the organization they want to partner with. Will you help them increase their revenue, decrease their expenses or do both? This will get their attention. Think of some ways to get your foot in the door for a one-to-one to start the relationship. Then it becomes about more than a business transaction. It is now about two people talking and building a relationship, and you have the chance to explain what you can do for them."

—*Supplier diversity professional with a large real estate organization, located in Danbury, Connecticut*

"It takes determination and follow-up, day after day. Work on your relationships. That's what will get you the contract. You will need lots of patience and lots of hard work. Have three to four targets to focus on, and be sure you are clear and concise in what you are selling."

—*MBE who matches minority-owned businesses with opportunities, located in Houston, Texas*

"Your sales effort has to be perpetual and continuous. Education is critical. It's important that you know what's happening in your industry and the marketplace and that you are dedicated to this."

—*Owner of a cargo transportation and logistics company, located in Houston, Texas*

"There are four key areas I believe minority business owners need to focus on. First is a vision. Have a winning vision. You need to select something that will be a magnet to potential customers. Something that distinguishes you from the rest of the crowd, a vision that is innovative and revolutionary, something that no one else has in the marketplace. Second is commitment. Commit to success. When you are alone, the road is very, very tough, and there are a number of bridges you have to cross. For those in a corporate structure the bridges are there. As a minority-owned company you have to build your own bridges. Success is tougher; the rewards are bigger, but the effort is tough. You must have a tremendous commitment to success. Third is cash management. This is critical because of all the unforeseen and irregular cash flows. Fourth is the packaging of marketing and networking. You may be the business owner but you are also the marketing agent. Your networking should be tactical and always looking for an opportunity. Be very selective on where you invest your money. You must be financially savvy and financially selective. Being small, you don't have the margin of error that a huge corporation has. When you invest you must know that you are recovering the investment dollars. Finally, ask yourself why minority and nonminority businesses win business. Focus, focus on the client to understand their challenges, their numbers, their procurement problem, and their issues. Become an expert on the client's issues, and be willing to delight them. With that approach you can conquer mountains. Procurement organizations think about which company they want to work with again and again. Your goal should be to become that company. If you conquer the heart of your client, that's the beginning of a huge success."

—*Former general manager of global procurement for a* Fortune 50 *corporation, currently an MBE providing quality control services, located in Houston Texas.*

"You must be diligent and always have an evolution of your business plan. You cannot be stagnant. Always look at how your services can change. Don't allow yourself to get too comfortable with your contacts."

—*Owner of an engineering and project management firm, located in Chicago, Illinois*

"Networking is key. Be an expert in what you do from top to bottom. Know your lane. Don't be afraid to help other MBEs. Sometimes opportunities may present themselves, but you may not be good in that area. Once you know what you know first, then you can then move into other areas."

—*Owner of a meat company, located in Nebraska*

"Ensure that your back office is in place to execute the work that you are going after. Commonly we see MBEs saying, 'Give me the work first, and I will figure out how to get it done.' Seldom does this work. Look at your execution strategy to ensure that you have the necessary capital and resources needed before you get the proposal. If you know the type of work you do, you should be able to scale to support future opportunities. Solicit the type of business to the magnitude that you can handle. You would then get repeat business as well as referrals. Do not overpromise to the point that you will not be able to deliver."

—*Owner of a technology firm, located in Houston, Texas*

"From a marketing and sales perspective, you should go for the 'no' as quickly as possible so you are not wasting time filling out registration forms from people who have no intentions of buying from you at all. Know your market, and know who is willing to spend the money it takes to bring you on board. To compete strictly on price is a losing proposition but to show the client the value you bring to the table and the return on their investment is critical. When you attend national trade shows and business expos there may be four hundred to five hundred firms, but in reality there may only be 20 to 25 percent that are actual ideal customers for you. If you try to spend ten minutes on all four hundred to five hundred, you would never get to the real opportunity."

—*Owner of a national janitorial and maintenance company, located in Greenville, South Carolina*

12
Executive-Level Insights on MBE Success

Reflections from the executive vice president of a minority-owned commercial real estate firm, located in Houston Texas

Having been raised within an entrepreneurial household, being an entrepreneur myself, and serving as counsel to many start-up and emerging businesses over the course of my career, I have often reflected upon what I consider to be the key attributes of successful entrepreneurs. My thoughts on this subject could be encapsulated in an oft-quoted proverb: If you want to go fast, go alone. If you want to go far, go with others.

Translate and transition the vision.

Consistent with most successful entrepreneurs I've encountered is the ability to translate their vision in order to effectively transition it into a comprehensive plan and subsequently into the implementation of strategic tactics. The vision, plan, and tactics derive from and build upon one another.

During the start-up phase of the business cycle, the founder of the business serves as the technical expert, rainmaker, and caretaker of client relationships. Principally fulfilling all of these roles over the long haul could stifle the growth of the business and is otherwise unsustainable. Those business leaders that are unable to offload one or more of these responsibilities are often unable to dedicate sufficient focus on the big picture of the business and its direction.

The successful entrepreneurs are those that, as leaders, can build capacity by attracting talent and strategic alliances that augment and advance the company's ability to enhance its technical expertise, develop and cultivate new business, and retain and grow client relationships. They must attract and empower talent who can take ownership for the success of their roles and projects, allowing the entrepreneurs to focus on the critical roles that they are most talented in or passionate about.

Strike the delicate balance between working on and working in the business.

It's often said that if you start a journey without a destination, you'll get there. Entrepreneurs often express angst about getting caught up in day-to-day business issues such as personnel matters and operational issues instead of being able to devote sufficient time to focus on big-picture and long-term initiatives that must be built upon incrementally. This complaint is consistently stated as "not being able to see the forest for the trees."

As leaders, successful entrepreneurs that I've been exposed to seem to be able to strike the delicate balance between the big picture and the day-to-day performance of their companies. There is no magic formula as to what that balance is, and I suppose it can vary based upon the business or industry and the skill sets of the entrepreneur. It likely varies also based upon the business cycle the company is in, whether it be the start-up phase, the growth phase, or the sustaining phase.

As a general proposition, at some time and at some point, the entrepreneurs I have observed have all managed to transition from being defined as a business owner to a CEO.

Have a singular focus, but don't forget about work/life balance.

One of the biggest misconceptions from those outside of the entrepreneurial environment is that entrepreneurs have autonomy such that they can work as much or as often as they want to. While it is true that they do not "punch a clock," the successful entrepreneurs I have seen along the way have universally been some of the hardest-working people I have encountered. Their businesses are not only what they do, but also a substantial part of who they are.

Successful entrepreneurs display a singular focus on their businesses. They are always "on." They eat, sleep, and drink the stuff. They are perpetually looking for ways to improve their business and themselves as business leaders. However, this common trait does not mean that they are one-dimensional in their approach to life.

Work/life balance is an extremely important objective for all the successful business owners I've known. The better entrepreneurs seem to be aware of the fact that they cannot allow themselves to operate in a silo in life. They apply the same characteristics that make them successful in business to the other aspects of their life. They take on their roles in their families, their communities, their charitable endeavors, and even their hobbies with the same dedication and passion. They realize that because they are such highly motivated and driven individuals, they must find avenues and time to refresh and renew themselves so that they can sustain their pace.

Find courage under fire.

I've heard it said that it's not that courageous people do not have fear, it's that they move forward in the face of their fears. This is a key characteristic of those entrepreneurs I have known to be successful. It takes courage to take on risk, manage through uncertainty, and overcome challenges.

The very nature of an entrepreneurial endeavor is risky. It is commonly known that more start-up businesses fail within three years than succeed. There are risks inherent in taking on debt, adding new personnel, expanding product or service offerings, and making infrastructure investments. In these instances and others, fear can paralyze or retard the pace of growth. Successful entrepreneurs are calculated risk-takers. They display an unquantifiable courage in their convictions based upon their research, preparation, and even instincts. They are imbued with a confidence and reasoned optimism that promotes buy-in from those they will need to count on to support their direction and strategy in order to result in a successful outcome.

This same convictional courage is displayed in times of uncertainty or challenge due to forces beyond their control. Successful entrepreneurs consistently display a steadfastness during times of feast or famine. A recession, the loss of an account, or a short-term setback does not cause them to alter their demeanor, personality, or leadership character. If the head is shaken, the body will fail. This consistent approach to the highs and lows results in confidence, dedication, and loyalty from those they are reliant upon to overcome challenges and emerge from uncertainty.

In a perfect world, I could predict who will become a successful entrepreneur, but I do not think it is a predictable science. In my view, successful entrepreneurs are a different breed of individual. Not better, but different. Intangible factors such as instincts, timing, and circumstance also play a role as well. Many technical components can be taught and learned. However, at the levels of integrity, character, and drive, one either has it, or they do not.

13
Even More Words of Wisdom from Minority Business Owners

"MBEs must understand their customers' different platforms. If we are talking to someone in the C-suite, there is a certain level of interest that needs to be communicated. As you present your offering, you would absolutely need to communicate and share it with supply chain managers, personnel, the operations group, the gatekeeper, and buyers and purchasers. There's a different message that needs to be communicated to each of them. They may all have different agendas and understandings. You need to know what those agendas are. Matching your solutions to what you do or choose to do will be key to your success. You cannot go into a C-suite conversation with a message appropriate for low-level purchasing managers. Understand the client and who you are pitching to, understand the organizational structure, and tailor your message accordingly."

—*Entrepreneur from Belleville, Michigan*

"Understand your business model. Most MBEs think we know how to make money. We try to get a contract, we mark it up, we produce a product or service, and then we bill the customer. That's not a business model. Understanding the business model is knowing how we make a profit, what the value proposition is, and what key resources we need to back the business. There are a number of questions associated with your business model. Understanding your business model will dictate how you behave in the market, what customers you leave alone, and what customers you go after. To be successful isn't just getting another contract. It's understanding your financing, what your financing can accommodate, and what your capacity is. People and the culture are important. The managers, leaders, and owners must really understand what they represent in the market. Most of us go into business with an 'I got to get a contract' attitude without really understanding all the pieces that go into the business. What type of financing do I need? What terms should I accept? What other resources do I need? Are these resources internal or do I outsource them? Do I hire directly? A lot of these questions we don't answer until much later in the process, and sometimes it's too late."

—*Large consulting firm*

"MBEs must become experts in their trade. They must enable themselves to be a resource for the clients, and not only have that knowledge, but also apply that knowledge. Your competitive edge is that you can be more agile than larger firms because you do not have the burden of the bureaucracy that larger firms have. This is an intrinsic value."

—*President of a minority business organization in Puerto Rico with thirty-one years of experience*

"Technology is the next thing. Any MBE that controls technology will be the one to lead in his or her industry. The ones that leverage technology in a way that show cost savings and address all the compliance and risk factors will be companies of the future, regardless of the business category."

—*Minority banking officer of a large financial institution, located in Charlotte, North Carolina*

"It is key that MBEs have a strong commitment and that they remain competitive, focusing on what they can do that's above and beyond their competitors and what they really bring to the table. They must be innovative and continuously look for the value-add. Find an industry target and penetrate that target. Don't allow yourself to go wide, but go deep. Instead of focusing the majority of your time on new customers, focus on your current customers, allowing them to be your true leaders, and they will do the work for you. You must differentiate yourself from the competitor and bring your value-add to the table with every phone call and every meeting. Be willing to walk away from business if it is not right for you or the client. Understand your passion, because your passion will drive you. That should be your center, regardless of outside influences. Remain flexible and always go the extra mile. Understand the critical impact of listening not to what you want to hear but to what your customer or potential customer is saying. Ensure that your goals align with their goals. They may not be able to use your product and services now; however, they may know someone that may need your product or services."

—Taken from a breakfast roundtable discussion with MBEs from sectors including retail manufacturing, technology, brand promotions, and IT staffing, as well as representatives from minority business development agencies and lending institutions

"MBEs must be clear about the services and solutions that their company offers. They must understand their value proposition and what that means and understand that their value proposition can change based on their clients or their clients' projects. You really have to understand what your client's or potential client's pain points are and their areas of growth and opportunities. When you talk with them, you can share your value proposition, so that you can mitigate and minimize the risk they see in doing business with you. You must be able to communicate to them how you will save them time, help them earn more money, or reduce expenses. Be very clear about differentiating yourself from your competition. Large entities often say that they can put all MBEs in a bag and shake them up and pull one out and get the same thing. How can you stand out, not just in your value proposition but also in the services that you offer that makes you different and can translate into success? There is a great quote from B. Smith in which she states you must be willing to stand on a mountain of 'noes' for one 'yes,' so the 'yes' is great, but it takes time to get there. Be patient and very diligent with the time it takes to get to the 'yes.' If you get a 'no,' don't give up. Work to establish that relationship. Don't become tone deaf. Don't take it personally. Take the time to understand why you got the 'no.' Find areas you can improve upon, and keep going and pushing so that no can become a 'yes' later. As a small business owner, your time is money. Educate yourself. Education is key to understanding where your gaps are and where you can get the resources you need so that you can scale and grow your business."

—*Owner of a project management consultancy firm, located in Houston, Texas*

"Be proactive. Participate in as many events as possible, networking to meet corporate clients. Follow up to find the opportunity that fits the need of the corporation and the minority company, and perform an exceptional job."

—*Owner of a printing company, located in Houston Texas*

> **Here are some questions to help you determine whether you are taking your company to the next level:**
> - Do you have financial success and flexibility?
> - Do you have the ability to attract top talent?
> - Do you have the ability to attract capital?
> - Are you sought out by others because of your market advantage?
> - Do you have a unique and clear value proposition?
> - Do you have evidence of your ability to compete in the free market?
> - Are you creating wealth?
> - Do you have a perpetuating business model?
> - Are you winning competitive industry awards?

"Network, network, network. Always follow up and get involved. Participate in and volunteer on committees. Get involved with leadership of various organizations. If you do this for free, customers and potential clients will have a very positive impression of you and your organization. Their thoughts in many cases are that if you do this for free, just think what you would do if they awarded you a contract. Sales is about having the customer trust you. It has nothing to do with business, it's about you."

—*Third-generation minority business owner, located in Florida*

"The top three things necessary to build a successful minority-owned business are:

1. Identify a strong value proposition within your organization.

2. Utilize and access networks such as the National Minority Supplier Development Conference.

3. Follow up! One of the most important things you can do is follow up and develop relationships. It may take years or a number of run-ins but those relationships will eventually pay off.

—*Corporate plus MBE*

"If you are a second-generation business owner or you recently decided to join the family business, it is important that you leverage current and new relationships and take advantage of every single educational opportunity. While creative disruption is important to push the business forward, it's just as important to have a deep understanding of how and where the company started, the current state of the company, and the direction in which your family and you want the company to go. Paying close attention to how things have been done, taking lots of notes, asking plenty of questions, thinking outside of the box, incorporating learned tactics to assist with productivity, having tough skin, being willing to take advice, planning, having a schedule, and being intentional with your days are all things that I find crucial to the continuation of a successful minority-owned business."

—*Second-generation commercial real estate business owner, located in Houston, Texas*

"It takes passion, dedication, creativity, and humility. Understand where you fit. Know yourself. Know your business and value proposition. Know your competition and distinguish yourself. Know when it's time to go."

—*Former president of a national minority supplier development organization.*

"As my Silver Fox Roundtable Coach states, expect the best, plan for the worst, and know what your 'why' is. Why are you doing what you do?"

—*Author Ed Ryland*

14
So What Are My Secrets to Success?

I start with the three foundational principles that, without question, have been responsible for my personal and business success. Regardless of the challenges I've endured, the losses I've had in both my personal life and my business, the successes, and the mountain-top experiences I've reached, three things have always been my guiding principles:

1. Staying spiritually fit.

2. Staying physically fit.

3. Staying mentally fit.

Spiritually, I do that by praying constantly and listening to God. Praying is when I'm talking to God, and I'm asking for his direction, guidance, and support. Meditation is when I'm listening to God's words, and I'm watching his actions while becoming enlightened. When I do that consistently, I can stay spiritually fit. Physically, it's mind over matter regardless of how I feel or don't feel. I have to push through my desire to want to just lie in bed or sit in that chair. So, I work out regularly. My routine is an hour-and-a-half workout five days a week. Working out helps me to take the body punches of life, so that when I feel weak I can still push through, especially when I'm overcoming an illness or a traumatic event. Sometimes I don't know how I will get through it, but being physically fit helps me put one foot in front of the other. Mentally, I committed myself at a very young age to immerse myself in knowledge and information, to be open minded, to read as much as I could about everything, and then to focus specifically on those areas of interest personally and for my career, and to continue to look for educational resources to take my knowledge and understanding to another level.

In the end success is how you define it. Don't allow anyone else to determine whether or not you are successful. You don't have to make a million dollars be successful. If you started and ran a minority-owned firm, you have been successful. Determine your own goal for success. If you have been able to provide for your family, you have been successful. If you have been able to contribute to the community, you have been successful. If you have made an impact or been an influence on others, you have been successful. If you have a great relationship with your family and friends and loved ones, you have been successful. If you have let go of resentment and anger and animosity that once stopped you from moving forward, you have been successful. You determine what success looks like.

So how do I start my journey to success? I always start with a plan and a vision. I know where I am today, but what's my vision for tomorrow? What's my vision for next year? What's my vision for the next five years? After reflecting upon my vision and what God wants me to do, I commit that to paper. If it's not committed to paper and a plan, it has less of a chance of coming to fruition. So, I start with a strategic plan. This plan is a dumping of ideas, strategies, and thoughts. Then I develop a 30-60-90 Day Action Plan so that I can stay focused on results for the next thirty days and not look at five years from now. **(You will find a place to write down your own 30-60-90 Day Action Plan at the end of this book.)**

There are plenty of books on how to be successful. I would suggest that you consider reading *How Successful People Think: Change Your Thinking, Change Your Life*, by John C. Maxwell. In his book he points out how to become a better thinker and highlights six points:

1. Expose yourself to get input. This includes reading books, reviewing trade magazines, and listening to tapes.

2. Expose yourself to and spend time with good thinkers. If you want to be a sharp thinker, be around sharp people

3. Choose to think good thoughts.

4. Act on your good thoughts. Ideas have a short shelf life. You must act on them before the expiration date. Think things through, then follow through.

5. Allow your emotions to create another good thought. Here, he states you can act your way into feeling long before you feel your way into action.

6. Repeat the process.

As MBEs we are constantly in a position of thinking about personnel, finances, marketing proposals, growth strategies, exit strategy, succession plans, legal issues, and relationships. The list goes on and on, and it is ever changing. It is critical that we develop action plans with deadlines to implement them with continuous follow-up to stay on track. While it's important to have plans, to be thought leaders, and to always be thinking about new, innovative ideas, two critical components of my success have been family and community. Engaging my family in the business has been extremely critical. They're the backbone and support when everyone else abandons you. They will continue to encourage you. My late wife was my biggest fan and biggest supporter. If I knew I had her support, that gave me extra strength and extra wind to keep moving. Family is critical, as is your community. I don't care how successful you are, unless you find a way to give back, your success will be limited and the happiness attached to your success will not be completely fulfilled. You must find a way to give back to help those who are hurting and less fortunate. The success that we have is not for me to buy a bigger house or more cars or more shoes. It's to provide for myself and my family and to help those who are truly less fortunate and in need.

15
Closing Thoughts

As I listened to the details of each MBE's story I, began to feel a deeper appreciation for all that each person had done to make building a successful MBE firm possible. Some of the comments drew deeper emotions from me. Several times I found myself evaluating my own story and journey, benchmarking my values and beliefs. These brave MBEs put it all on the line, opening doors and breaking ceilings that never should have existed. Their words and wisdom sometimes came across like a gentle giant and sometimes like a roaring storm. They spoke as if they had a secret weapon, something bigger than themselves that was saying, "Keep going. You can do this." And they probably did. It's their shoulders that we stand on, their pain and challenges that help others avoid the same, their determination that drives us, and their fulfilled visions that keep us dreaming. As an MBE, never lose sight of the dream and the vision that you held so closely for yourself and your family. Their struggles and eventual successes should remove every doubt you may have of failure. Their words and actions should empower you to ignore the naysayers and divorce yourself from those who stand in your way. The strength of these MBEs should bring an end to any thoughts of giving up or disappointment of an unmet goal. Their outlook on life inspires hope and passion to be the best. It should terminate the existence of mediocre, replacing it with greatness. You can now draw from a wellspring of knowledge and faith as you analyze your business, your life, and your future. I know you will use the answers found here to ponder what makes these MBEs so special.

Is it their hard work, commitment, talent, faith, love of community, perseverance, or commitment to excellence? Just what is it? Maybe, just maybe, it's all of the above.

When things don't turn out the way you plan or envision, give thanks anyway. God has something bigger and greater in store for you. It may not look like it as things are developing. There may be holes or gaps in your fence, but God may be saying, "I want to let a little sunlight shine through. I want to let a little encouragement shine through. I want to let a little hope shine through." Keep pushing. In the end, if you have been faithful to your higher power and faithful to your craft, you will be amazed at how much better things will turn out.

There is a wonderful book I read called *When All You've Ever Wanted Isn't Enough: The Search for a Life That Matters,* by Harold Kushner. He asked the question, "Are we asking too much of life when we say, 'All I want is to be happy?'" Is happiness like eternal youth and perpetual motion—a goal that we are not meant to reach no matter how hard we work for it? Or is it possible for people to be happy, but we are going about it the wrong way? He mentions a quote from Oscar Wilde, who wrote, "In this world there are only two tragedies. One is not getting what one wants, and the other is getting it." As you read the words of the successful minority business owners in this book, contemplate your own business success. You may want to ask a similar question. As a minority business owner, we put a lot of blood, sweat, tears, and years into starting, running, and building a successful business, but at what cost? Is it worth your health, or your relationships with spouses and significant others or family members? There should be a healthy balance between striving to be a successful minority business owner and understanding your personal happiness. As Harold Kushner points out, oftentimes we can never rest and enjoy accomplishments. We need one new success after another and constant assurance from people around us to still the voice inside of us to keep us sane. One of the main things we strive for is to know that our lives matter, that our communities will be better as a result of our involvement. Be careful not to spend all of your youth and your mature years focused totally on building your business and, in the end, find yourself sick, lonely, and afraid. The happiest people are not always the richest. You become happy by living a life that means something. Be careful that the overwhelming desire for wealth and power does not separate you from other people. Living solely for yourself never brings complete satisfaction; only living for others will help you accomplish that. You now have quite a bit of information regarding building a successful business, but remember this: you may have a lot of information but never using it is like having a hundred guitars and never taking a music lesson or strumming the strings. Make a commitment to not just read what is being shared, but also to implement it into your business and your life. Don't let your story be only that of a person who made a lot of money, got a lot education, made a lot of friends, and went to a lot of parties. Be sure your life adds up to more than that. Never allow yourself to stop caring about the quality of your work, which leads to a corrosive spirit. We all dream of the perfect world, the perfect marriage, the perfect children, and perfect clients. When that does not happen, we may feel like failures. We have to be careful here that we don't continuously measure our real-life achievements against our happiness.

I wish you twenty-four hours of success that is multiplied forever.

All the Best,

Ed Ryland, CCIM, MCR

President and CEO, ARVO Realty Advisors

Book Ed Ryland for Speaking Engagements or Events

If you would like for Ed to be a guest speaker or participate in any of your events please visit his website, www.EdRyland.com, or contact:

Tiffany Ryland

(832) 549-6490

tiffany.ryland@arvorealtyadvisors.com

Instagram: @Tiffany.Ryland

LinkedIn: Tiffany Ryland

Facebook: Tiffany Ryland

Or

Ed Ryland

(832) 689-0617

ed.ryland@arvorealtyadvisors.com

Instagram: @Ed.Ryland

LinkedIn: Ed Ryland, CCIM, MCR

Facebook: Ed Ryland

Your Notes and Action Plan

NOTES TO TAKE MY BUSINESS TO THE NEXT LEVEL

NOTES TO TAKE MY BUSINESS TO THE NEXT LEVEL

NOTES TO TAKE MY BUSINESS TO THE NEXT LEVEL

30-60-90 DAY ACTION PLAN

DATE	ACTION PLAN	RESPONSIBLE PARTY	DEADLINE

30-60-90 DAY ACTION PLAN

DATE	ACTION PLAN	RESPONSIBLE PARTY	DEADLINE

30-60-90 DAY ACTION PLAN

DATE	ACTION PLAN	RESPONSIBLE PARTY	DEADLINE

30-60-90 DAY ACTION PLAN

DATE	ACTION PLAN	RESPONSIBLE PARTY	DEADLINE

30-60-90 DAY ACTION PLAN

DATE	ACTION PLAN	RESPONSIBLE PARTY	DEADLINE